# ANNI'S DIARY OF FRANCE

For Maria, Zoe
and family.

SPAIN

A TRELD BICKNELL BOOK

Published by Whispering Coyote Press, Inc.
480 Newbury Street, Suite 104
Danvers, Massachusetts 01923

Printed in Singapore by Imago Publishing.

10  8  6  4  2  1  3  5  7  9

**Library of Congress Cataloging-in-Publication Data**

Axworthy, Anni.
   Anni's diary of France / by Anni Axworthy.
     p.   cm.
   "A Treld Bicknell book"—T. p. verso.
   Summary: Anni's diary describes the trip to France that
she takes with her mom and dad.

ISBN: 1-879085-58-5 : $14.95

   [1. Diaries—Fiction. 2. France—Fiction.] I. Title.
II. Title: Diary of France.
PZ7.A9616Am 1994
[Fic]—dc20

                93–27278
                    CIP
                    AC

Text set in Souvenir Light
by The R & B Partnership

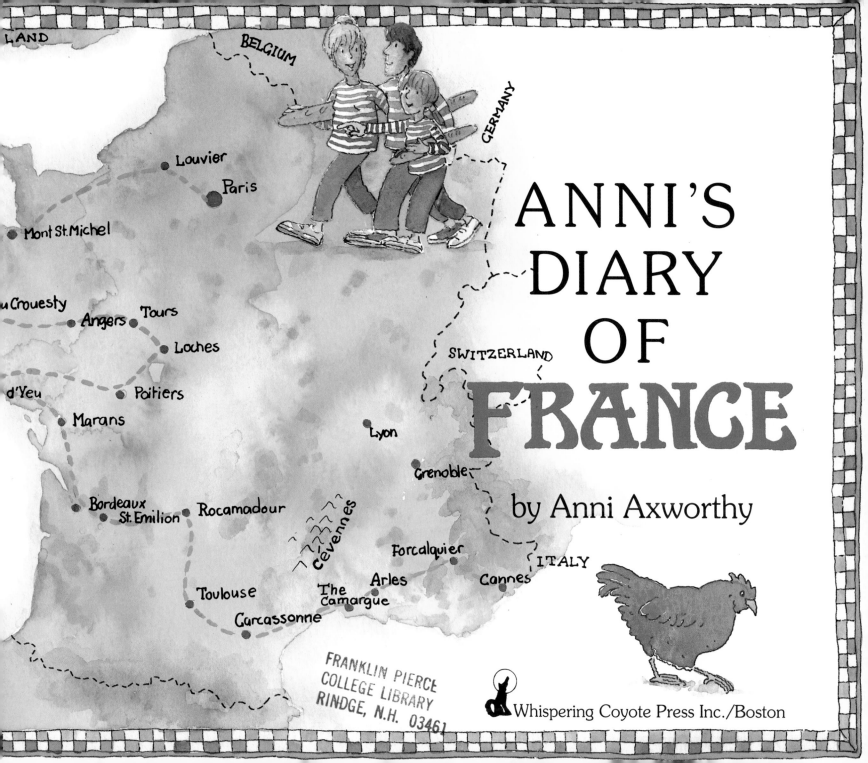

ANNI'S
DIARY
OF
FRANCE

by Anni Axworthy

Whispering Coyote Press Inc./Boston

LAND

BELGIUM

GERMANY

Louvier

Paris

Mont St. Michel

u Crouesty

Angers  Tours

Loches

d'Yeu

Poitiers

Marans

SWITZERLAND

Lyon

Grenoble

ITALY

Bordeaux  Rocamadour
St. Emilion

Cévennes

Forcalquier

Arles

Cannes

Toulouse

The
Camargue

Carcassonne

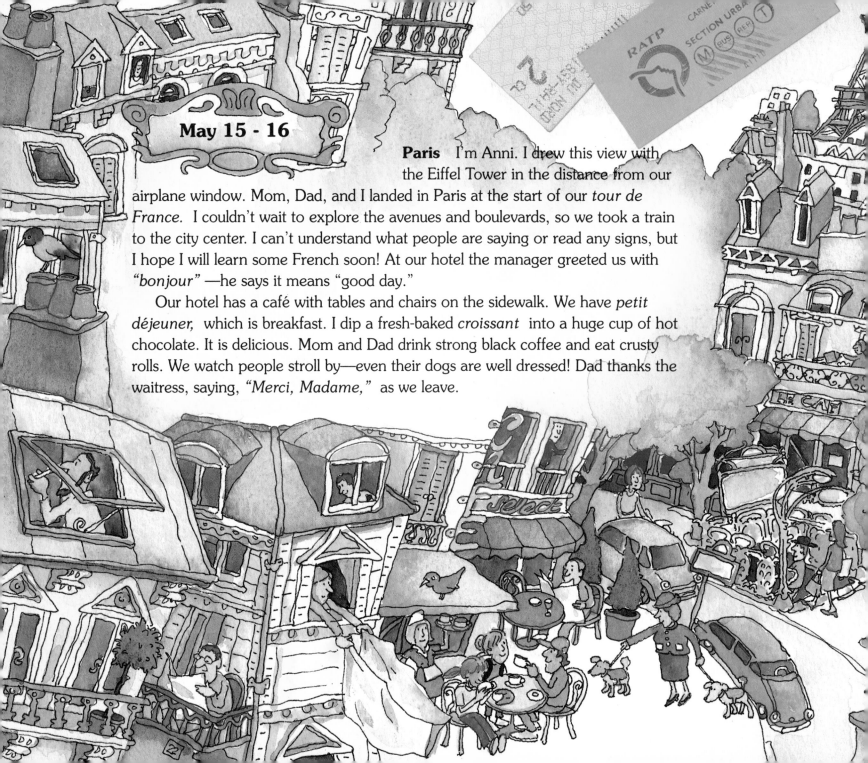

**May 15 - 16**

**Paris**   I'm Anni. I drew this view with the Eiffel Tower in the distance from our airplane window. Mom, Dad, and I landed in Paris at the start of our *tour de France.*  I couldn't wait to explore the avenues and boulevards, so we took a train to the city center. I can't understand what people are saying or read any signs, but I hope I will learn some French soon! At our hotel the manager greeted us with *"bonjour"* —he says it means "good day."

Our hotel has a café with tables and chairs on the sidewalk. We have *petit déjeuner,*  which is breakfast. I dip a fresh-baked *croissant*  into a huge cup of hot chocolate. It is delicious. Mom and Dad drink strong black coffee and eat crusty rolls. We watch people stroll by—even their dogs are well dressed! Dad thanks the waitress, saying, *"Merci, Madame,"*  as we leave.

SEINE

ILE DE LA CITÉ

ILE ST-LOUIS

The statue of Liberty was a gift from the French people to the Americans in 1886.

Liberté 1886-1986

RÉPUBLIQUE FRANÇAISE

The Paris subway is called the Métro; it was built for the visitors to the Paris World Fair in 1900. There are 100 miles of track and 430 stations. Some of the entrances are designed in the curly *Art Nouveau* style—I think they look like plants.

We take the Métro to the Île de la Cité, an island in the river Seine. This is where Paris began, but then it was called Lutetia by the Romans. In front of us stands the beautiful Cathedral of Notre Dame. It took two hundred years to build and is almost nine hundred years old! I look up at the carved stone figures above the doors. They were made to help people who couldn't read understand the stories of the Bible. Inside the cathedral, hundreds of candles send flickering shadows over the stone walls. High above our heads the sun shines brilliant blue through the huge, round, stained-glass windows.

We cross the Pont Neuf, which means new bridge but it is really the oldest bridge in Paris. Along the banks of the Seine people sell old books, maps, prints, and postcards from big boxes with hinged lids and doors. Mom and I choose postcards while Dad buys a long bread roll—called a *baguette*—and cheese *(fromage)* for our picnic lunch.

*Up in the bell tower we share a rooftop view of Paris with gargoyles. I make a face to look like one, too.*

May 17

UNION
DES ARTS
DECORATIFS
PALAIS DU
LOUVRE
107 - RUE
DE RIVOLI
PARIS 1er
1411177

TARIF RED

079463 B
Ministère de la Culture
C.N.M.H.S.
DROIT D'ENTRÉE
31 F
Plein Tarif
A prés. à toute exposition
C.N.M.H.S. - Plein Tarif
Droit d'Entrée 31 F.
079463 B

0660200048

Union
des Arts
Décoratifs

USÉE

We make an early start so there will be time to see some of the four hundred thousand works of art at the Palais du Louvre—one of the biggest museums in the world. It was originally built as a fort and later became a palace, but it has been an art gallery for two hundred years. In 1987 a huge glass pyramid and fountains were added to form a new main entrance. I love the way the clouds and blue sky are reflected in the glass. We visit just one corner of the Louvre, the Union des Arts Decoratifs. Inside are beautiful objects and whole rooms from the past. We leave Mom gazing at wallpaper with painted palm trees and statues. I think she is getting ideas for our living room at home. A grand marble staircase leads to a wonderful exhibition of toys. Dad searches for his favorite train set among the teddy bears, tin cars, building blocks, and dolls.

During lunch we imagine we can each choose one gift from the Louvre. Mom picks the painting of the *Mona Lisa* by Leonardo da Vinci, but I think I'd prefer the toy camel made from corrugated cardboard in the toy exhibition.

We explore the crowded bustling streets of the "Left Bank." Everything smells different and exciting. The long Boulevard St. Michel leads to Montparnasse. Near the Métro station we go down a spiral staircase into the catacombs. These underground tunnels, made by quarrying for rock, were used to store bones from all the cemeteries of Paris. Mom reaches for my hand when we pass a sign that says: STOP, BEYOND HERE IS THE EMPIRE OF DEATH. Stacked on either side of the path are hundreds of bones and skulls, glinting gold in the dim light.

Dad wants to visit a few more ghosts in the Montparnasse cemetery. Mom and I find the giant statue of a cat and, close by, a family of wild cats which have set up home among the miniature temples, stone angels, and urns.

*On the way home we hear music—it's a marionette singing in the Métro!*

**May 18**

We have come to see one of the most-visited buildings in the whole of France, the Centre Georges Pompidou for Art and Culture in the Rue Beaubourg. It looks like it has been turned inside out. All the pipes are colorcoded: blue for air, green for water, yellow for electricity, and red for heating. Outside, jugglers, mime artists, and fire-eaters perform. I try to sit still while a street artist draws a caricature of me. Then I make a drawing of him, too. He says it is *"très bien,"* which means very good.

The escalator to the gallery goes up through a clear tube on the outside of the building. We take it to the fifth floor for a rooftop view of Paris. Below us we can see the wonderful funny fountains in the square.

Mom says we cannot leave Paris, the fashion capital of the world, without visiting at least one department store. We go to the famous Galeries Lafayette. While she chooses a hat, I look up at the incredible, domed, stained-glass ceiling five floors above.

Dad says that because Paris is also the food capital of the world we must fit in a visit to Place de la Madeleine, where the best *gourmet* grocery shops are found. Fauchon's shop is like a dream come true: feather-light pastries, chocolates marked with golden letters, the finest coffee and tea from around the world, fat lobsters bubbling away in tanks, and shelves of exotic bottles and jars. They even have Champagne mustard!

We end our stay with a huge farewell dinner of *fruits de mer,* a mixture of delicious seafood. Our waiter wishes us, *"bon appetit!"*

REPUBLIQUE FRANÇAISE 0.65 POSTES H. MATISSE

I love Matisse!

Boulangerie
Pâtisserie
**M. FORTIN**
PARIS 10e

**May 19**

**Normandy** We leave the city behind and drive through the countryside, past apple orchards and thick forests, orange farmhouses and pretty cream-colored cows. Our *petit* car is called a *deux chevaux* (it has just "two horses"). The canvas roof rolls back so we can see, hear, and smell everything.

Dad is eager to stop for lunch—this is where soft Camembert cheese, cider, and *calvados* (apple brandy) come from. I go to explore the sleepy streets of Louvier while Mom and Dad recover from our *déjeuner* in the public gardens. Behind the eight-hundred-year-old cathedral I spot a giant yellow butterfly on the side of a building. Walking closer, I see there are flowers and patterns made from broken china all over the house. It is very strange! Every inch of wall is studded with china, mirrors, seashells, plates, and fairy-tale statues.

I rush back to get Mom and Dad. When we reach the door, we are greeted by an old man with a smiling face and a beautiful blue sweater who invites us to come inside his home. It is just as amazing as the garden. It is truly *La Maison de la Vaisselle Cassée*—a house of broken crockery.

**May 20**

**Mont St. Michel** Just off the coast of Normandy stands the small, magical island of Mont St. Michel. It hasn't always been an island and was once surrounded by forest. In 708, a bishop called Aubert was told in three dreams to build a church on top of its rocky peak. Many pilgrims came to visit the church. Then, one day, a huge tidal wave swept over the land, destroying the forest and turning Mont St. Michel into an island only reachable during low tides. Quicksand, and a tide which rushed in faster than a galloping horse, made the journey very dangerous for the pilgrims. An order of monks came and settled there, and for nine hundred years the island was built upon. The local people called it *La Merveille*—The Marvel. At last a causeway was added, connecting it once more to the mainland.

As I wander around, I pretend to be one of the monks who lived in this beautiful abbey. It was built on the highest point of the island so that it was close to heaven. It looks very near to me as the sun pours like silver through the magnificent windows high above our heads. I love the peaceful cloisters—a small garden surrounded by rows of stone pillars carved with plants and flowers. They are a perfect place for the monks to pray and meditate.

It's good to be Anni again, outside in the sunshine. We follow in the steps of the pilgrims of the past, choosing souvenirs in the *La Grande Rue* before leaving.

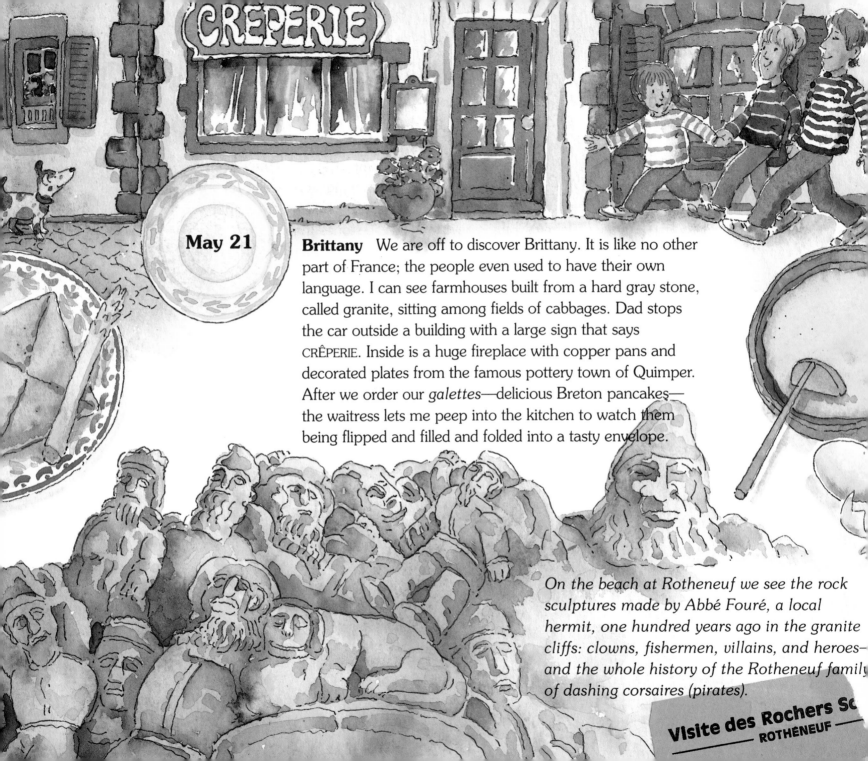

**May 21**

**Brittany** We are off to discover Brittany. It is like no other part of France; the people even used to have their own language. I can see farmhouses built from a hard gray stone, called granite, sitting among fields of cabbages. Dad stops the car outside a building with a large sign that says CRÊPERIE. Inside is a huge fireplace with copper pans and decorated plates from the famous pottery town of Quimper. After we order our *galettes*—delicious Breton pancakes— the waitress lets me peep into the kitchen to watch them being flipped and filled and folded into a tasty envelope.

*On the beach at Rotheneuf we see the rock sculptures made by Abbé Fouré, a local hermit, one hundred years ago in the granite cliffs: clowns, fishermen, villains, and heroes— and the whole history of the Rotheneuf family of dashing corsaires (pirates).*

Visite des Rochers Sc
ROTHÉNEUF

**May 22**

menhir

dolmen

algotherapie

**Carnac**  The ancient stones of Carnac date back to 4000 or 5000 B.C., making them older than the Egyptian pyramids. Rows of standing stones—more than three thousand of them—stretch for nearly a mile. Many scholars have studied the stones trying to discover their purpose; some people believe that they were used to measure the distances between the stars.

Before leaving Brittany, Mom suggests that we visit the Hotel Miramar for a seawater treatment called by the wonderful name of Thalassotherapy. These soothing and healing treatments were invented by the ancient Greeks and became so popular in France that centers were built all along the coast. It feels wonderful lying in a bath of warm, bubbling seawater, breathing in the salty air. Afterward my skin is coated with a green paste made from sea algae. I look and smell like a sea monster. It is washed away with first warm and then cold seawater. Mom and Dad say that I have never looked so clean. It feels great!

ALIGNEMENTS DE CARNAC  1.00
POSTES  REPUBLIQUE FRANÇAIS

PORT CROUESTY
HOTEL MIRAMAR

**May 25th**

Emblem of François I

**The Loire**  The kings and queens of France chose the Loire Valley in which to build their magnificent *châteaux* because it was near to Paris, and its fertile fields and forests were perfect for farming and hunting. We follow the Loire, France's longest river, hoping to visit some of the *châteaux*.

REPUBLIQUE 0.45
POSTES
SULLY-sur-LOIRE

We have found a *gîte* in a *château*. Madame and Monsieur B and Countess, their French spaniel, welcome us and show us to our rooms. Mine has a giant four-poster bed and a little bathroom in a round tower. I feel just like a Princess.

Countess leads the way down a grassy slope to the river. A grass snake slithers across the path; Madame says that they are harmless. We push aside the reeds and climb into a flat-bottomed boat. Dad takes the oars and steers us along the river. Then it's my turn to row. I try not to splash Mom and Dad too much, but it is hard. Coypus with whiskery faces rustle in the reeds as we pass.

**May 27**

Emblem of Louis XII

In the distance I can see white towers resting among the shadows of the forest of Chinon. Mom's guide book says that this is the Château de Rigny-Usse. I can understand why it was the inspiration for the story *Sleeping Beauty!* The guide shows us rooms with heavily draped four-poster beds and cabinets with secret drawers. In the hallway we see a massive pair of men's riding boots. Perhaps they belonged to Prince Charming?

Angers  *Tapestries of the Apocalypse woven in wool and gold thread.*

**Angers**

**Nantes**

Loire

Saumur  *Known for its mushroom caves, fine wines, and cavalry school.*

**Saumur**

In the courtyard we climb up a tower marked with a sign *La Belleau Bois Dormant*—The Beauty of the Sleeping Wood. It leads to a walkway where we peer into rooms showing scenes from the whole story of the fairy princess and the wicked sorceress. Dad breaks the spell by pointing out the view of the river and, below us, Mom waving from the flower garden.

Saumur
APPELLATION CONTROLEE

Cuvée du Patron

Loire

Amboise   *We saw the Maison de Enchantment, a collection of moving puppets: Dr. Jekyll and Mr. Hyde, a fashion parade, and Beauty and the Beast.*

Tours

...ndry   *Famous for its ...ture of Italian and ...ch garden design.*

Amboise

Cher

Langais   Villandry

Chenonceaux

Azay le Rideau

Usse

chinon

Loches

Indre

Chenonceau   *Stands reflected in the river Cher, sheltered in the forest. It was designed by women.*

Azay-le-Rideau   *It is built on an island on the Indre River and has boats on the moat.*

Vienne

Creuse

Chinon
APPELLATION CONTROLEE

Cave des Roches
Touraine
Appellation Touraine Control
Embouteillé par Michel Parade Loches

CHATEAU DE CHENONCEAU
Propriété Privée

VILLANDRY
Plein Tarif
Jardins

VILLANDRY
Tarif Réduit
Jardins

**May 30**

**Loches**  We are staying with a French family in Loches, in the Loire Valley. From their house we can see the *château* and the dungeon. It was used as a prison until 1927. Dad says I better behave!

Their daughter Angela is twelve years old; she is going to take me to her *école*—that is school. Perhaps I will learn some new French words. Morning lessons begin at eight o'clock, and each one lasts for forty-five minutes. It is a Catholic school and some of the classes are taught by monks from the nearby monastery. I like the English and art lessons best. At twelve-thirty the pupils go home for lunch. Many French families try to share a meal at this time of day. The school day ends at five o'clock.

The village of Villaines les Rochers is known for baskets. Didi helps his father to lay the wicker to dry before it is tied into neat bundles, ready for the basketmakers. They can make all kinds of things: baskets, bowls, boxes, and even tables and chairs.

On the way home we visit a farm famous for its goat's milk cheese called *chèvre*. The farmer is proud to show us the cool dairy where racks with hundreds of white logs and pyramids of cheese are maturing. Some have already been covered with ashes ready for market. Angela leads me to the barn where sweet-smelling goats look up from their mangers of clover to wish us *bonsoir*.

Angela and I set off to collect the salad. We knock on a small wooden door set into the cliff wall. Windows and a smoking chimney poke from the grassy clifftop. There are many houses built into the soft limestone caves of the Loire Valley. This is the home of a *troglodyte*. The caves stay at the same temperature in summer and winter, and are good places to grow mushrooms *(champignons)* or store wine. With a warm fire they make cosy places to live.

Marcel comes to the door carrying a huge ginger cat. He proudly shows us the garden where he grows tidy rows of vegetables, an aviary of white doves, and a waterpump hiding a nest with a tiny egg. He helps us to pick fresh crisp lettuce and collect a bouquet of herbs.

**June 5**

**Futuroscope**   Here we are at Futuroscope, a theme park of the moving image. Kinemax looks like a massive crystal growing out of the earth. Inside it has a cinema screen as tall as a seven-story building. In Omnimax a movie about fire is projected into a giant dome. I feel like I am right there among the flames and smoke. After that we need a cold drink.

My favorite show of all is called *Le Tapis Magique*—the Magic Carpet. We follow a butterfly's journey from Canada to Mexico on a huge screen. Suddenly, on the glass floor we can see the butterfly's view of the ground as it crosses oceans, deserts, and mountains. Phew! My wings could do with a rest.

In the 3-D cinema everyone wears special glasses that make the animals in the movie look so real that I even tried to stroke a lion.

Dad gets soaked in the water maze, but Mom and I stay nice and dry on our floating water scooters. We have one last thrill at *Le Cinéma Dynamique*. It feels just as though we are riding the bobsled on the screen. Wind blows in our faces and the seats rock from side to side. It is great! I can hear Mom screaming louder than anyone else. This is one of my favorite days!

**Île d'Yeu**   Last night I curled up on deck under a star-freckled
sky and listened to the throbbing engines and the sea gulls following
the ferry which took us to the Île d'Yeu, a small island off the coast. Now
it is a beautiful morning. From the window I can see rows of brilliant white cottages
with shutters painted all colors of the rainbow.

There are few roads or cars on the island so we have chosen a bicycle each.
Mine has a basket for my diary and paintbox. Our first stop is for breakfast at the
harbor. A fisherman tells me the French word for boat is *bâteau*.  Wild flowers and
yellow butterflies flit past our wheels. This is wonderful! We leave our bikes on the
cliff top and scramble down the rocks to a golden beach. Among the seaweed-
covered rocks, I discover a little turquoise lagoon. Mom holds my
clothes, I count *"un, deux, trois,"* and jump in! *Il fait froid*—it is
cold! Dad says mine is the loudest scream he has ever heard.

At Port de la Meule we share an enormous bowl of *moules*
(mussels)—it is big enough to feed the whole island! I try using a shell
as a tweezer to pluck out the tasty morsels. A mountain of bread
comes in handy to mop up the creamy broth from our plates. Yum!

The ferry is waiting for us at Port Joinville. I wave goodbye
to the *Île de Couleur,*  my new name for the island.

**June 10**

**Marais Poitevin** used to be a huge swamp. In the thirteenth century, monks dug canals and, free from the threat of constant floods, people began to farm the fertile land. Everything was carried on flat-bottomed boats—even cows and horses. We hire a boat and float away from the busy roads and bridges. Yellow broom and willows grow along the banks. Only a pair of ducks with a fluffy family of chicks are in a hurry. A heron stands knee deep, his gray business suit reflected in the water, waiting for his *déjeuner* to swim past. It is my turn to steer the boat; it only takes one hand. I can wave *bonjour* to the fishermen snoozing beside their rods and picnic baskets.

Coiffe de Marans.

**June 11**

**St. Emilion** We are following in the footsteps of Emilion, an eighth-century monk who came from Brittany to the Bordeaux region. He settled in a humble cave and became known as a miracle worker. It is easy to guess the real reason why Dad insists that we visit the medieval town of St. Emilion. It is surrounded by mile after mile of gentle, sloping vineyards, with more than a thousand *châteaux,* which are famous all over the world for their fine wines.

We stay in a family-run inn, called an *auberge,* in the center of town. Nearby is the Eglise Monolithe. It is a church carved from a single massive rock, by monks, in memory of St. Emilion.

Dad leads the way along a pathway through the vineyards. Rose bushes, planted to encourage bees to pollinate the vines, mark the end of each row. The farmers are busy all year—pruning and burning dead wood in the fall, weeding and tying up young shoots in the spring, spraying and weeding in the summer. Finally, between September and October, the grapes are harvested.

We visit a cave where the wine is made. The *vigneron* (the wine grower) tells us that grapes are the only fruit to have both sugar and yeast, the ingredients needed to make alcohol. Mom and Dad taste glasses of wine made in different years so that they can choose which one to buy. The *vigneron* gives me a glass of *cassis* made from black currant to try during *la dégustation,* the tasting.

**June 12**

**Rocamadour**    Today we are making the same journey that pilgrims have made for hundreds of years. The town of Rocamadour clings to the side of a cliff, high above the Alzou Canyon. It is amazing! It grew from a small village to a town after a body was found under a chapel. When it was laid next to the altar, a series of miracles began to happen. Many pilgrims, including royalty, came to visit the site. Mom says it is not a good idea for me to climb the 100 steps to the Chapel of Notre Dame in the style of the pilgrims of old—on their hands and knees and tied with chains. Inside, the walls and ceiling are black with the soot of years of burning candles. Sailors have hung up miniature ships as reminders of their prayers to keep them safe at sea.

We climb a zigzag track to the cliff top. It is hot and we are grateful for the shade from the over-hanging trees. At the top is a *château* built to defend the pilgrims over the years. Looking down from the ramparts, I can see birds flying over orange rooftops and people moving in the streets below like ants.

Hôtel Ste-Marie
★★
RESTAURANT -- BAR

Serge et Martine CASARIN
46500 ROCAMADOUR
en QUERCY
Téléphone :
Fax. 65 33

ROC-AMADOUR

**June 15**

CARCASSONNE 5F

...ouse is the perfect place for people-
...hing. It is full of students and
...shops and sidewalk cafes. We have a
...ese dinner and stroll through the still-
...streets.

**Carcassonne** is a real medieval walled city. It once lay on an important trade route between the Atlantic Ocean and the Mediterranean Sea, close to Spain. From early times, bitter battles have been fought over it. Two thick surrounding walls with towers protect the city. From here soldiers threw spears and catapulted rocks at the invaders attacking from below.

Exploring the narrow streets it is easy to imagine life in the thirteenth century. A chicken appears from a garden gate and crosses our path, and a lady strolls by with a basket of bread. It is hard to imagine, on a lazy sun-baked afternoon, those battles fought on the walls of Carcassonne.

**June 20**

**The Camargue** is a triangle of marshland between the Rhone and the Petit Rhone rivers and the Mediterranean Sea. Cowboys, known as *gardiens,* have lived and worked here since 1572. They ride the famous white horses and raise the small black bulls used throughout southern France for bullfights called *cocardes,* after the cloth rosette which is attached to a string tied between the bull's horns. When the bull enters the arena, the *razeteurs,* dressed in white, try to remove the rosette from his forehead with a hook. But often the nippy animals chase the men from the ring, even jumping over the barrier after them.

Louis is a *gardien;* he says the best way to see the Camargue is on horseback. We ride "Americana"—using western saddles with long stirrups and holding both reins in one hand. The reeds surrounding a muddy pool rustle with startled birds as we pass; a brilliant blue kingfisher darts across our path. Wild horses knee-deep in salty mud squelch about, grazing on the marsh grass. Set among the marshes are the homes of the *gardiens* called *cabines*—single-story bungalows with thatched roofs. Louis says that they are always built with the door facing south to avoid the strong winter wind, called the *mistral.*

**June 21**

**Arles** Dad is walking bow-legged and Mom has a sore bottom. I don't think they would make very good cowboys. Our dinner in the ancient town of Arles is served with rice grown in the paddy fields of Camargue and salt mined in the nearby town of *Aigues-Mortes* (known as the city of the dead waters). The Romans turned this little fishing port on the banks of the river Rhône into a bustling town.

Arles became the home of the Dutch painter, Vincent Van Gogh. The beautiful town, surrounded by avenues of plane trees and fields of sunflowers, inspired him to paint many of his most famous works of art. It is inspiring to me, too!

BAR

VILLE d'ARLES
Monuments et Musées Muni
Musée Réattu

**June 25-28**

**Provence** Through a green tunnel of plane trees, we drive past fields of glowing red poppies, blue-green juniper trees, and silver rocks that shimmer in the sunshine. No wonder many of the Impressionist painters set up their easels and recorded the unique colors of Provence.

Tonight we are cooking dinner for everyone, so we come to the market at nearby Forcalquier. All French towns have at least one market day each week. Farmers set out their local produce on tables in roads and courtyards. Mom and Dad fill the basket with artichokes and melons and stop to choose olives—there are ten different types. I look after Rabu, the farmer's dog. He leads me to a shady square and, while he takes a cool drink at the fountain, I buy some *cerises,* cherries. I find Dad in another shady courtyard where he has joined a group of men playing *boules.* Each player has three metal balls which they throw in turn at a small ball called the "jack." The winner is the owner of the ball nearest to the jack. Rabu tries to join the game, but changes his mind when he feels how heavy the *boules* are.

**June 29-30**

**Cote d'Azur** We are on our way to the seaside, driving past pretty hilltop villages set among olive groves. Cannes, with its broad avenues, sparkling sea and luxury hotels like giant wedding cakes, is quite a contrast. We stroll under the palm trees of the Promenade de la Croisette, which runs alongside a beach crowded with sun beds and matching parasols. Maybe we'll see a movie star visiting the International Film Festival held in Cannes each summer. Vendors push carts of ice cream past, we cannot resist the refreshing *citron glace*.

At last we find a quieter *plage* (beach) and soak off the city dust in the warm blue sea. Dad swims up and down. He says he is working up an appetite for another lavish seafood supper.

**July 1**

**The Cévennes** In 1878 the Scottish writer Robert Louis Stevenson trekked across the wooded hills of central France, accompanied by Modestine, a small donkey "…. not much bigger than a dog, and the color of a mouse."

The book he wrote about his journey is called *Travels With A Donkey in the Cévennes*.

Sunbathing lizards dart from the guiding stones which mark the pathway, as we hike along a part of Stevenson's 120-mile route. We are glad to reach the shady alleys in a village built of gold-colored stone with low flat roofs. The sound of clanking bells and hoofs on hard ground warn us of the arrival of a herd of goats, pursued by a shepherding dog. As they pass a man from the village collects the manure. He explains that it is *"pour le jardin, Madame."* He brings a tray of cool drinks and tells us that the goats are going to a meadow with a stream. I ask if I can go, too.

*The saucisse (sausage) van.*

*Wild flowers attract butterflies—there are meadow browns, adonis blues, marbled white, swallowtails, orange tips, and hundreds of fritillaries.*

0.10 TIMBRE-TAXE RÉPUBLIQUE FRANÇAISE POSTES

1,00 TIMBRE-TAXE RÉPUBLIQUE FRANÇAISE POSTES

We are staying in a tall, dark house with stone tiles on the roof. The downstairs room is used as the cellar; there are logs and boxes of vegetables, jars of bottled fruit and dried mushrooms and, hanging from the ceiling, bunches of dried herbs. Madame leads up the steep stairs to the kitchen; the smell of lavender wafts through the open window. She shows us old photos of her family, the women in long skirts and wooden clogs. The village looks just as it did one hundred years ago.

Mom and Dad's room has wooden steps which lead up to my room. From the window I can see villagers tending their hillside gardens and, in the distance, blue woods and purple mountains. The bird song is so loud that I can't sleep! I tiptoe out past Mom and Dad. Madame is also an early riser. We share a *petit déjeuner* on the terrace. She tells me that the other singing I can hear is the *cicadas*—large, winged insects which make their song by bending their stomachs back and forth. I try it, too, but all that I hear is Madame's laughter.

Soon it is time to trek back to the car and the twentieth century. Dad suggests we find a donkey to carry the bottles of wine that the villagers presented to him. I ask if we can call her Modestine.

## July 5

Dad is trying to find space in his backpack for several bottles of wine; he says they will remind him of the places we have visited. Mom can hardly lift her pack; it is so full of pots and pans—even a *crêpe* pan from Brittany. The gypsy basket is stuffed with pottery, and jars of honey from the Loire Valley, and small bottles of scent—her memories of Provence.

We spend our last few hours in France in a typically French way. Each course of our dinner is memorable. I can still taste the *mousse au chocolat* when we climb onto the plane. As we soar above France, we lift our glasses to toast all the French people who have become our friends and made us so welcome in their magnificent country.

*Au Revoir La France!*

## DATE DUE

| SEP 0 8. '97 | | | |
|---|---|---|---|
| MAR 2 9 2004 | | | |
| | | | |
| | | | |
| | | | |
| | | | |
| | | | |
| | | | |
| | | | |
| | | | |
| | | | |
| | | | |
| | | | |
| | | | |
| | | | |
| | | | |
| | | | |
| GAYLORD | | | PRINTED IN U.S.A |

# Glossary

**Art Nouveau** — style of drawing developed in France in 1890's, with curving lines and featuring stylized flowers and leaves

**Auberge** — a family-run inn or small hotel

**Au revoir la France** — literally, "till I see you again, France"—Goodbye France

**Baguette** — long stick of French bread

**Bâteau** — boat

**Bon appétit** — literally, "good appetite," meaning enjoy your meal. There is no directly equivalent phrase in English

**Bonjour** — good-day, the greeting of the day, used like "hello" in English

**Bonsoir** — good-evening, the greeting of the evening

**Boules** — a popular game played all over France, using three metal balls and a small white ball called a "jack." People often play boules in the main square

**Cabines** — single-story houses with thatched roofs where the *gardiens,* or cowboys, of the Camargue live

**Calvados** — apple brandy from a region in France called Calvados

**Cassis** — a fortified wine made from blackcurrants

**Cerises** — cherries

**Champignons** — mushrooms

**Château(x)** — a castle(s)

**Chèvre** — goat; goat's cheese

**Cocardes** — rosettes worn by the bulls at bullfights in southern France; the bullfight

**Corsaire** — a pirate

**Couleur** — color

**Crêperie** — place where *crêpes* are made and sold. *Crêpes* are thin pancakes cooked in a special pan

**Croissant** — crescent-shaped pastry made with butter and usually eaten for breakfast

**Déjeuner** — lunch, to have lunch; *petit déjeuner* breakfast

**Deux chevaux** — name of a small French Citroen car which literally means "two horses"

**École** — school